WEREWOLVES

by
Rebecca Phillips-Bartlett

Minneapolis, Minnesota

Credits

All images are courtesy of Shutterstock.com, unless otherwise specified. With thanks to Getty Images, Thinkstock Photo, iStockphoto, and Adobe Stock.

Recurring – M.KOS , Alex Ghidan, Dychek Marina. Cover – delcarmat, klyaksun, SpicyTruffel. 4–5 – Mia Stendal, Q88, RIMM_Art, losw. 6–7 – GSoul. 8–9 – rudall30, DanieleGay, albertogagna, Marsha Harris, jsteck. 10–11 – DomCritelli, rudall30, StuPorts, GSoul, JM-MEDIA. 12–13 – Denis---S, Declan Hillman, Lili Kudrili, rbv, Dimitris66. 14–15 – Warpaint, Se_vector, Diana Jo Marmont, BONNIE WATTON, gregglmt, Valerii Maksimov. 16–17 – Holly Kuchera, Andrii Zastrozhnov, BONNIE WATTON, Volodymyr TVERDOKHLIB, Guppic the duck. 18–19 – delcarmat, Hoika Mikhail, matiasdelcarmine. 20–21 – DanieleGay, vovan, Taras Khimchak. 22–23 – len4foto, wavebreakmedia, Przemek Klos, UfaBizPhoto.

Bearport Publishing Company Product Development Team
Publisher: Jen Jenson; Director of Product Development: Spencer Brinker; Managing Editor: Allison Juda; Editor: Cole Nelson; Associate Editor: Naomi Reich; Associate Editor: Tiana Tran; Art Director: Colin O'Dea; Designer: Kim Jones; Designer: Kayla Eggert; Product Development Specialist: Owen Hamlin

Library of Congress Cataloging-in-Publication Data

Names: Phillips-Bartlett, Rebecca, 1999- author.
Title: Werewolves / Rebecca Phillips-Bartlett.
Description: Fusion books. | Minneapolis, Minnesota : Bearport Publishing
 Company, 2025. | Series: Mythical creatures | Includes index.
Identifiers: LCCN 2024035370 (print) | LCCN 2024035371 (ebook) | ISBN
 9798892327428 (library binding) | ISBN 9798892327923 (paperback) | ISBN
 9798892328296 (ebook)
Subjects: LCSH: Werewolves--Juvenile literature.
Classification: LCC GR830.W4 P45 2025 (print) | LCC GR830.W4 (ebook) |
 DDC 398.24/54--dc23/eng/20240802
LC record available at https://lccn.loc.gov/2024035370
LC ebook record available at https://lccn.loc.gov/2024035371

© 2025 BookLife Publishing
This edition is published by arrangement with BookLife Publishing.

North American adaptations © 2025 Bearport Publishing Company. All rights reserved. No part of this publication may be reproduced in whole or in part, stored in any retrieval system, or transmitted in any form or by any means, electronic, mechanical, photocopying, recording, or otherwise, without written permission from the publisher.

For more information, write to Bearport Publishing, 5357 Penn Avenue South, Minneapolis, MN 55419.

CONTENTS

Myths, Magic, and More. **4**

What Does a Werewolf Look Like? **6**

A Dangerous Beast **8**

Super Senses. **10**

This and That **12**

Becoming a Wolf. **14**

Where Werewolves Live **16**

Mythical Look-Alikes **18**

Real-Life Werewolves? **20**

Mysterious Mythical Creatures **22**

Glossary **24**

Index **24**

MYTHS, MAGIC, AND MORE

Most people have heard of the powerful, furry creatures known as werewolves (WAIR-wulvz). But you probably haven't seen one in real life. Why not? Because werewolves are **mythical** creatures.

For thousands of years, people from all around the world have told stories about werewolves. Different **legends** talk about the creatures in different ways. Let's learn what the stories have to say!

The word *werewolf* comes from two old English words that mean *man* and *wolf*.

WHAT DOES A WEREWOLF LOOK LIKE?

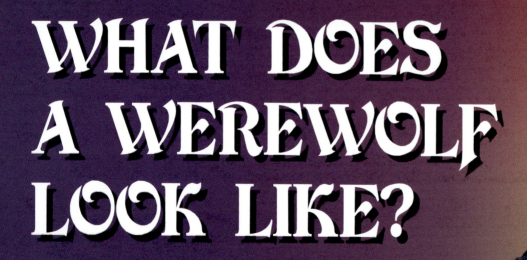

Let's take a look at these hairy beasts.

Fur

Thick fur covers their body from head to toe.

Legs

In legends, werewolves can walk on two sturdy legs. Sometimes, they are said to run on all fours.

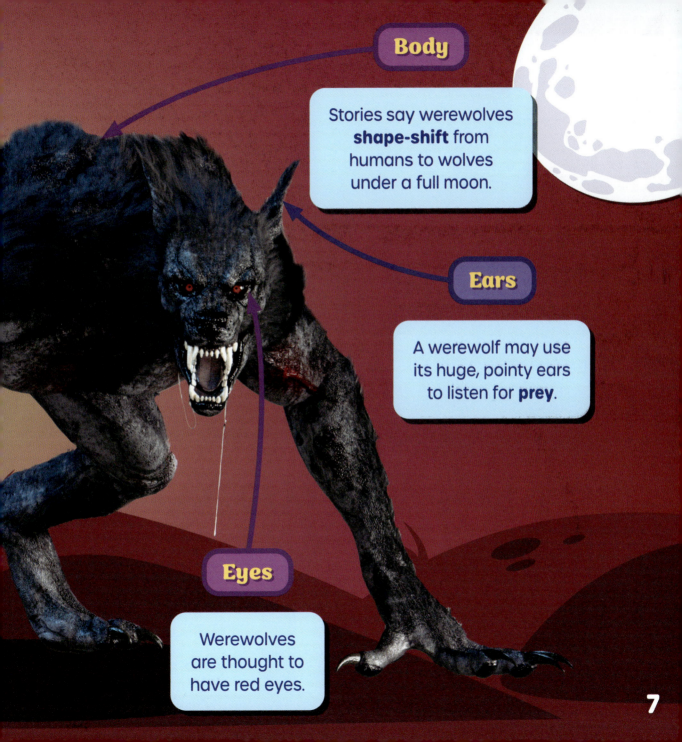

Body

Stories say werewolves **shape-shift** from humans to wolves under a full moon.

Ears

A werewolf may use its huge, pointy ears to listen for **prey**.

Eyes

Werewolves are thought to have red eyes.

A DANGEROUS BEAST

Werewolves are known for attacking and eating other creatures. How do they do this? They use their long claws and sharp teeth!

In stories, these beasts cannot control themselves while in their wolf forms. They are said to hunt down any living thing and to use their long claws to attack.

Werewolves in stories have sharp teeth called canines. Humans have canines, too. But werewolf teeth are said to resemble those of wolves, bears, or lions.

Canines

A wolf's canines

Some werewolves in legends are thought to become vampires after they die.

SUPER SENSES

Apart from incredible strength, what else have we heard about these mythical creatures? Werewolves have super senses!

Many stories say werewolves have a strong sense of smell. Could they even smell fear? Dogs know when someone is scared or nervous because of the smell of their sweat.

Werewolves are also thought to be able to run at amazing speeds. The fastest land animals on Earth are cheetahs. Could werewolves be even faster? Who knows!

Cheetahs can run as fast as 70 miles per hour (110 kph).

THIS AND THAT

In **myths**, people turn into werewolves after being bitten or scratched by the beasts. Some say it starts from a **curse**.

Werewolves are believed to shape-shift during a full moon. A full moon occurs about once a month. It lasts up to three days.

A full moon

In popular media, humans who turn into werewolves suffer from memory loss. They do not remember what happened in their wolf forms. They may get hurt, but they may not even remember how!

BECOMING A WOLF

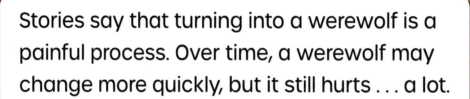

Stories say that turning into a werewolf is a painful process. Over time, a werewolf may change more quickly, but it still hurts . . . a lot.

That's why some myths claim that werewolves look for something to stop the shape-shifting. Wolfsbane is a herb that is believed to stop werewolves from changing during a full moon. For humans, this plant can cause death.

Wolfsbane

The herb is called *wolfsbane* because it was once used to **poison** wolves.

WHERE WEREWOLVES LIVE

Most werewolves in stories live in mountains and forests. These faraway places help the beasts lurk around at night without being spotted.

Could werewolves be living among us? Maybe they spend most of their days as humans. But once a full moon rises, the monstrous beasts come out.

MYTHICAL LOOK-ALIKES

There are other mythical creatures like werewolves. Let's look at a few.

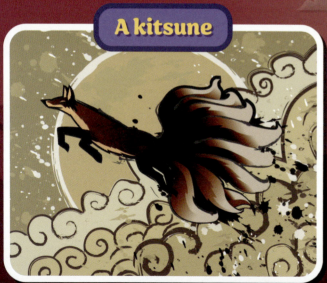

A kitsune

Kitsune (KIT-soo-nay) come from Japanese myths. They are foxes that can shape-shift into humans.

In stories, Cerberus (SUR-buh-ruhs) was a large dog with black, shaggy fur. Like werewolves, Cerberus had beady red eyes. But this terrifying beast had three heads instead of just one!

Cerberus

In Greek myths, Cerberus kept watch over the **underworld**.

REAL-LIFE WEREWOLVES?

Where do stories of werewolves come from? Maybe from real animals....

Dogs

There are more than 300 different dog breeds. Some dogs look like werewolves because of their furry coats.

Wolves

Wolves are often mistaken for werewolves when they are seen at dawn or dusk. These animals usually live in groups called packs.

MYSTERIOUS MYTHICAL CREATURES

Werewolves are fun, mysterious creatures. We can learn a lot from stories about these terrifying beasts.

If you can't get enough of werewolves, just read some books! There is so much to learn about these magical, mythical creatures.

23

GLOSSARY

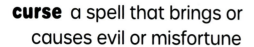

curse a spell that brings or causes evil or misfortune

legends stories from the past that may have a mix of truth and made-up things

mythical based on stories or something made up in the imagination

myths old stories that tell of strange or magical events and creatures

poison something that can hurt or kill a living thing if eaten or touched

prey an animal that is hunted and eaten by other animals

shape-shift to change from one physical form into another

underworld the place where some people believe that dead people go

INDEX

curses 12–13, 15
eyes 7, 19
full moon 7, 13, 15, 17
fur 4, 6, 19, 21
humans 7, 9, 13, 15, 17

prey 7–8
shape-shift 7, 13, 18
teeth 8–9
vampires 9
wolfsbane 15